MW01245635

COOPERATING

ALTERNATIVES TO COMPETITION IN THE HOME AND CLASSROOM

Written by **Mary Anne McElmurry, O.P.**

Illustrations by **Darcy Tom**

Cover by Darcy Tom

ISBN No. 0-86653-334-6

Printing No. 98765432

GOOD APPLE, INC.
BOX 299
CARTHAGE, IL 62321-0299

Description of
Kino Learning Center

Kino Learning Center is a private, nonprofit elementary and secondary school founded in Tucson, Arizona, in 1975 by parents seeking an alternative learning environment for children. The school is staffed by 20 teachers and has an enrollment of 200 students between the ages of 3 and 18.

At Kino Learning Center the students, teachers, and parents form a learning community in which people are bound together in mutual aid, responsibility and cooperation. Freedom exists within this interaction as the liberty persons grant to each other out of their faith in and concern for one another. Such freedom is nourished by mutual respect and appreciation; from it, trust grows and individuality flourishes.

Within the prepared learning environment of the school, each child is free to choose from worthwhile options, a sequence of activities unique to his/her needs and experiences, in which he/she finds success, interest, and pleasure. Each child is free to develop in the way and at the pace appropriate to his/her needs, abilities, and interests. The school places special stress on individual discovery, on firsthand experience, and on creative work.

At Kino Learning Center, adults and children mutually engaged in the learning process are continually in the process of changing and growing, for to learn is to change. And to experience joy in learning is to delight in life itself, for learning and life are one.

ACKNOWLEDGEMENTS

Thank you to the students and teachers of Kino Learning Center who have generated the ideas for this book through their cooperation with one another. Special thanks to Mary Jane Cera for creatively critiquing the activities in this book, to Sandy Webb for typing the manuscript, and to Joyce Smith for proofreading the final product.

INTRODUCTION

Many critics of modern society point to the loss of a sense of values as a major cause of contemporary problems. While the blame is often placed on the young and teenaged, all age levels seem to have shifted away from an awareness of where they are going. Today's youth are highly criticized for a behavior which reflects a lack of respect for self and others, a general disregard for people and things. There is a drastic need for adult America to assist its youth to deal with the innumerable areas of confusion and conflict in our modern society. The need for the development of a positive self-image and a value system consistent with one's beliefs and behaviors is a vital part of one's existence and survival.

Values can best be developed through questioning one's own feelings and behaviors as well as discussing and responding to the feelings and behaviors of others. Values can also be developed through making decisions in an atmosphere that allows many choices, invites relevant questions, and encourages respect for self and others.

The development of values must be seen as a lifelong process which recognizes changing circumstances rather than a fixed set of unyielding principles. Rather than reacting to a predetermined, fixed moral code, youngsters must be encouraged to develop a self-determined value system which reflects a respect for self, others, and things.

It is the teachers of a school who set the tone and create the atmosphere that is so necessary and appropriate to value education. Their approach to life, their feelings and responses toward themselves and others, and their attitudes toward all living things and the environment have a profound influence upon the attitudes and behavior of their students. It is in this warm, accepting atmosphere that students are invited to develop a tolerance, acceptance, and genuine concern for themselves, others, and living and nonliving things.

Teachers must create innumerable activities and situations which, while developing skills in academic areas, at the same time lead a child toward a basic understanding and development of humaneness. Helping children to become concerned and actively involved in finding solutions to problems in a cooperative manner is an important aspect of values development.

The activities in this book are designed to assist students to improve their relational skills by better knowing and appreciating themselves, as well as people close to them and throughout the world.

The activities in this book are designed to assist students to become more cooperative individuals and to demonstrate increased cooperation within their families and school communities.

As the activities in this book are completed, students will have the opportunity to define cooperation for themselves and to evaluate the degree to which they integrate cooperation and competition into their lives. Students will also determine their family values and identify the qualities possessed by various family members. Students will be asked to identify quality time within their family life and will be challenged to create more quality time together. Students will be asked to identify how they cooperate with their school community. They will recognize the strengths they bring to the group as well as the qualities of their classmates. Students will be asked to participate in various cooperative games and to evaluate their degree of enjoyment. Finally, students will be challenged to apply their cooperation skills to solving problems that will create for themselves a preferable future of local and global unity.

As the activities in this book are completed, students will have repeated opportunities to affirm each other's uniqueness, capability, and cooperation. This need for a positive self-image, a clearly defined values code, and consistent cooperative beliefs and behaviors is vital for today's youth as they begin to hold a more constructive and positive view of themselves and their world. Herein lies the challenge of the present moment and the hope for all that is worthwhile for generations to come.

PURPOSE OF BOOK:

The purposes of the activities in this book are to help you:

- become a more cooperative person.
- better cooperate with your family.
- better cooperate with your friends and classmates.

Before beginning the activities in this book, complete the following statements by putting a check (✔) in the box that best describes you.

	Usually	Often	Sometimes	Seldom	Never
I am a cooperative person.					
I cooperate with my family.					
I cooperate with my friends and classmates.					

Name _____

Date_____

1

PART ONE: BECOMING A COOPERATIVE PERSON

PURPOSE:

The purpose of the activities in **PART ONE** is to assist you in becoming a more cooperative person.

Before beginning Part One, complete the following statement:

I am a cooperative person:

☐ usually.

☐ often.

☐ sometimes.

☐ seldom.

☐ never.

Name _____

Date _____

1. DEFINING COOPERATION

- Write ten words inside the box that best describe what **cooperating** means to you. Use some of the words listed if you like. Use some of your own words not listed below.

winning

sharing

giving in

supporting

monopolizing

teaming

joining

arguing

listening

compromising

defending

conversing

losing

- Circle the word from your list that best describes what cooperation means to you.

COOPERATING MEANS

_____

_____

_____

_____

_____

_____

_____

_____

_____

2. BEING COOPERATIVE

- Listed below are several qualities of a cooperative person. Put a star (✱) in front of the qualities that you strongly possess.

_____ **supportive** (approving; encouraging)

_____ **listening** (hearing; understanding)

_____ **open-minded** (willing to listen to new ideas)

_____ **responsible** (being in charge of one's own actions)

_____ **accepting** (welcoming of people and their ideas)

_____ **warm** (friendly; kind; affectionate)

_____ **curious** (eager to get information and knowledge)

_____ **persevering** (committed to finishing what I start)

_____ **concerned** (interested; involved)

_____ **enthusiastic** (eager; excited)

_____ **tolerant** (respectful of the rights and opinions of others)

_____ **communicative** (talkative)

> supportive
> listening
> warm
> curious
> concerned
> enthusiastic
> ...me!

- Circle one quality that you wish you possessed to a greater degree.

- Tell what you could do to increase this quality in your life.

_____

_____

_____

_____

_____

_____

- You may want to put your plan for growth into action.

3. KNOWING MYSELF

You need to know yourself before you can cooperate with others.

- List the five most important qualities you bring to a relationship.

_____

_____

_____

_____

_____

- Put a star (✱) in front of the most important quality you possess as a person.

4. LIKING MYSELF

- Pretend that you have purchased a want ad in the newspaper. Advertise yourself as a good friend. Tell why people might like to have you for a friend.

IN NEED OF A FRIEND?

5. TAKING A RISK

- Honesty and trust are two important qualities that help bring about cooperation. It is important for you to be honest about who and what you are. It is equally important to believe that who and what you are is acceptable to others.

- Describe who and what you are in the space below. Take the risk to tell about your hopes and fears, your strengths and weaknesses, your dreams for the future, etc.

6. CHOOSING TO BE POSITIVE

Most people like to be around and work with people who have positive attitudes about themselves.

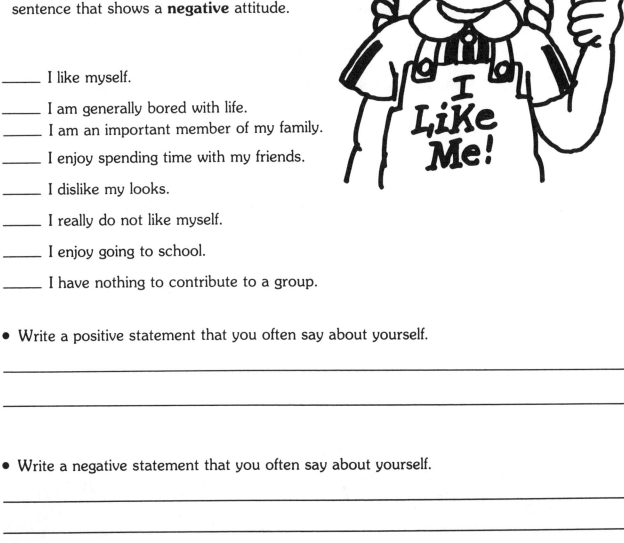

- Put a **P** in front of the sentence that shows a **positive** attitude. Put an **N** in front of the sentence that shows a **negative** attitude.

_____ I like myself.

_____ I am generally bored with life.

_____ I am an important member of my family.

_____ I enjoy spending time with my friends.

_____ I dislike my looks.

_____ I really do not like myself.

_____ I enjoy going to school.

_____ I have nothing to contribute to a group.

- Write a positive statement that you often say about yourself.

_____

_____

- Write a negative statement that you often say about yourself.

_____

_____

You may want to:
- Try to think about yourself in positive rather than negative ways.
- Try to talk about yourself in positive rather than negative ways.

7. UNDERSTANDING MYSELF

• Put an **X** on the line that indicates how you generally relate with other people.

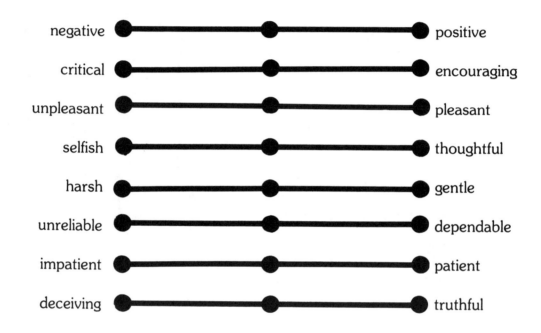

negative ●━━━━━●━━━━━● positive

critical ●━━━━━●━━━━━● encouraging

unpleasant ●━━━━━●━━━━━● pleasant

selfish ●━━━━━●━━━━━● thoughtful

harsh ●━━━━━●━━━━━● gentle

unreliable ●━━━━━●━━━━━● dependable

impatient ●━━━━━●━━━━━● patient

deceiving ●━━━━━●━━━━━● truthful

• Write your own opposite terms that describe how people relate. Indicate how you relate on the lines below.

8

8. WORKING WITH OTHERS

- Put an **X** on the line that usually describes your degree of cooperation with others.

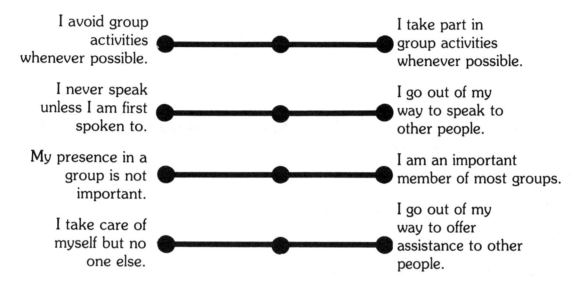

I avoid group activities whenever possible. ●━━━━●━━━━● I take part in group activities whenever possible.

I never speak unless I am first spoken to. ●━━━━●━━━━● I go out of my way to speak to other people.

My presence in a group is not important. ●━━━━●━━━━● I am an important member of most groups.

I take care of myself but no one else. ●━━━━●━━━━● I go out of my way to offer assistance to other people.

- Make up your own cooperative sentences. Put an **X** to indicate your degree of cooperation.

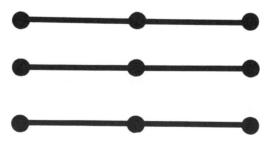

9. SETTING GOALS

goals?

In order to be cooperative in a group setting, it helps to state your goals before participating in a group activity.

- State a cooperative goal for each activity listed below.

> **Example:**
>
> Activity: **family picnic**
>
> Goal: **to watch the baby so that Mom and Dad can have a relaxing time**

Activity: **movie with friends**

Goal: _____

_____

Activity: **lunch with grandparents**

Goal: _____

_____

Activity: **friend's birthday party**

Goal: _____

_____

Activity: **class discussion on fighting**

Goal: _____

_____

- State your own cooperative activity and goal below.

Activity: _____

Goal: _____

_____

_____

10. ACCOMPLISHING GOALS

Listed below are three reasons why people might want to cooperate with one another in an effort to accomplish a specific goal.

- Read each statement. Number the statements in their order of importance for reaching goals in a cooperative manner.

_____ When people work together, less time is needed to accomplish the goal than when people work separately.

_____ When people work together, more creative solutions to a problem can be found than when people work separately.

_____ When people work together, a higher quality job can be accomplished than when people work separately.

- Give your own reasons for working with other people to accomplish a goal rather than working alone.

_____

_____

_____

_____

_____

_____

_____

_____

_____

_____

11. COOPERATION *vs.* COMPETITION

- If the sentence describes **cooperation,** draw a line to that word.

- If the sentence describes **competition,** draw a line to that word.

> "Let's work together so we can get our jobs finished quickly."

> "Let's play hard, but let's play fair."

> "When our team gets far enough ahead, the bad players can have a turn."

> "Let's think of a game we can play together."

- Write a **cooperative** sentence you say often.

_____

_____

_____

- Write a **competitive** sentence you say often.

_____

_____

_____

12. TAKING A STAND

- Circle the sentence in each box that best describes your feelings and actions.

a. I play games to win.
b. I play games for fun.
c. I play games both for fun and to win.
d. I do not play games.

a. I enjoy playing with friends.
b. I enjoy playing with myself.
c. I enjoy both playing by myself and with friends.

a. I like to play team sports.

b. I like to watch team sports.

c. I like to both play and watch team sports.

d. I neither enjoy playing nor watching team sports.

a. I am basically a competitive person.

b. I am basically a cooperative person.

c. I possess a balance between cooperation and competition.

- Discuss with your classmates how you are a competitive person.
- Discuss how you are a cooperative person.
- Discuss ways your class might become a more cooperative group.
- Put your plans for cooperation into action.

13. PICTURING COMPETITION

- Find pictures and words that describe competition. Paste your clippings in the space below to make a collage.

- You may want to cut out your individual collage and add it to a larger classroom collage on competition.

14. PICTURING COOPERATION

• Find pictures and words that describe cooperation. Paste your clippings in the space below to make a collage.

• You may want to cut out your individual collage and add it to a larger classroom collage on cooperation.

15. ENJOYING MYSELF

- Name three of your favorite sports on the lines below.

- In the boxes, describe each sport as either **COMPETITIVE** or **COOPERATIVE**.

_____

_____

_____

- Name three of your favorite games on the lines below.

- In the boxes, describe each game as either **COMPETITIVE** or **COOPERATIVE**.

_____

_____

_____

16. DESCRIBING MYSELF

- Tell how you are a **competitive** person in the space below.

- Tell how you are a **cooperative** person in the space below.

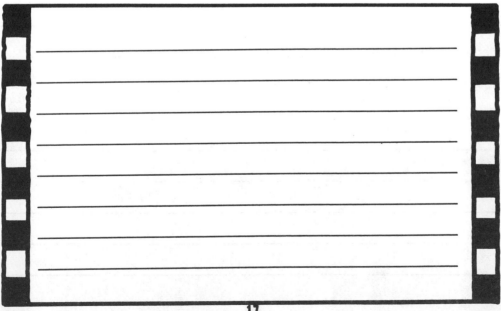

17. COOPERATING WITH OTHERS

- Listed below are some groups with whom you relate. Number each group (1 to 6) according to the importance of each in your life.

_____ parents

_____ grandparents

_____ brothers, sisters

_____ cousins

_____ classmates

_____ neighbors

- Put a star (✱) in front of the group with whom you best cooperate.

- Tell how you cooperate with these people. _____

_____

_____

_____

- Put a check (✔) in front of the group with whom you least cooperate.

- Tell how you might better cooperate with these people.

_____

_____

_____

_____

_____

_____

18. MAKING A DIFFERENCE

• Name some specific things you can do to better communicate with your family.

• Name some specific things you can do to better communicate with your teacher and classmates.

19. SYMBOLIZING COOPERATION AND COMPETITION

A star is a symbol of success. An eagle is a symbol of freedom. Design symbols for competition and cooperation in the circles below. Tell about your symbols in the spaces provided.

20. QUOTING COOPERATION

Below are quotes that describe cooperation.

- Write your own quote in the space provided.
- Share your motto with your classmates.

"The more we get together, the happier we'll be."

"Two heads are better than one."

SUMMARY PART ONE: BECOMING A COOPERATIVE PERSON

Cooperating means

_____

_____

_____

Choose one:
I am generally
- [ ] a competitive person.
- [ ] a cooperative person.
- [ ] both competitive and cooperative.

Choose one:
I am generally
- [ ] a positive person.
- [ ] a negative person.
- [ ] both positive and negative.

Three qualities that make me a cooperative person are:

_____

_____

_____

Check the box that best describes you.	Usually	Sometimes	Seldom
I enjoy group activities.			
I enjoy talking to people.			
I enjoy being alone.			
I play games to win.			
I play games to have fun.			
I cooperate with people.			

Name _____   Date _____

PART TWO: COOPERATING WITH MY FAMILY

PURPOSE:

The purpose of the activities in **PART TWO** is to assist you in becoming a more cooperative person with your family.

Before beginning Part Two, complete the following statement:

I cooperate with my family:

- ☐ usually.
- ☐ often.
- ☐ sometimes.
- ☐ seldom.
- ☐ never.

Name _____

Date _____

21. MEASURING UP

- Check the appropriate box for each of the statements.

Members of My Family	Usually	Sometimes	Seldom
Spend quality time together.			
Pitch in and do the housework.			
Talk openly and listen attentively.			
Set rules and try to live by them.			
Work out problems as they arise.			
Enjoy being with each other.			

- You may want to discuss with your family how to improve one of the characteristics listed above.

- You may want to put your plan for improvement into action.

22. DETERMINING VALUES

Values are people, things, ideas, events, etc., that you care about.

- Determine as a family those things you most value.

- List your family values in the space provided.

_____	_____
_____	_____
_____	_____
_____	_____
_____	_____
_____	_____
_____	_____

- Put a star (✳) in front of the item your family values most.

- Tell why this item is of value to you and your family.

_____

_____

_____

_____

_____

_____

_____

_____

_____

23. COUNTING ON ONE ANOTHER

- Write the name of the family member who best fits the description below.

I can count on _____ to make me laugh.

I can count on _____ to play with me.

I can count on _____ to help me with my schoolwork.

I can count on _____ to answer my questions.

I can count on _____ to help with the housework.

I can count on _____ to plan a party.

I can count on _____ to repair something broken.

I can count on _____ for a tasty meal.

I can count on _____ to listen to my problems.

I can count on _____ to keep a secret.

I can count on _____ to _____

- My family can count on me to:

_____

_____

_____

_____

_____

_____

_____

_____

_____

_____

_____

_____

COUNT ON ONE ANOTHER

24. SAYING THANKS

Fill out, decorate, and cut out the award below. Give the award to a family member whom you can really count on.

I can count on you!

To: _____

For: _____

_____

From: _____

Date: _____

25. COOPERATING AT HOME

- List several things in your home that you share with other members of your family.

telephone	_____
bathroom	_____
_____	_____
_____	_____
_____	_____

- Choose one item. Tell how you cooperate with other family members by sharing this home item.

_____

_____

_____

_____

_____

_____

28

26. PITCHING IN

- Listed below are some common family activities. Tell how you cooperate with each activity.

a. **cleaning the house**

_____

_____

_____

b. **preparing the meals**

_____

_____

_____

c. **getting ready for a holiday**

_____

_____

_____

d. **resolving an argument**

_____

_____

_____

e. _____

_____

_____

_____

27. SPENDING TIME TOGETHER

- Discuss with your family those activities you most enjoy doing together.

- List five activities your family most enjoys doing together.

  a. _____

  b. _____

  c. _____

  d. _____

  e. _____

- Put a dollar sign ($) in front of those activities that require more than $5 for the entire family to enjoy together.

- Put a star (✻) in front of the activity your family most enjoys.

- Put a check (✔) in front of the activity you most enjoy personally.

- Put an **O** in front of those activities you do often, that is, at least once a week.

28. PLANNING AHEAD

Does your family value spending quality time together?

• You may want to use the schedule below to plan cooperative time together.

• Mark the activity and the time in the space provided. Try to plan at least one activity for each day.

SUNDAY _____

_____

_____

MONDAY _____

_____

_____

TUESDAY _____

_____

_____

WEDNESDAY _____

_____

_____

THURSDAY _____

_____

_____

FRIDAY _____

_____

_____

SATURDAY _____

_____

_____

• Make a sincere effort to complete each family activity you plan.

29. BREAKING TRADITION

Most American families spend several hours a day gathered around their television sets. Try breaking this American pastime.

- Plan a family evening of entertainment without television.

- Tell about the evening below.

- Evaluate the evening by answering the following questions.

My family enjoyed the evening:	My family plans another such evening in the near future.
☐ a great deal.	☐ Yes
☐ somewhat.	☐ No
☐ not at all.	☐ Maybe

30. ENJOYING FAMILY READING

Discuss with your family the possibility of planning a family reading time.

- If you agree with this goal, you will have to determine when, what, and who will read.

- Tell about your family reading experience in the space provided.

(lined space for writing)

- Be patient with yourselves. It may take some time to successfully integrate family reading into your life and home.

- Share your family reading experience with other members of your class.

31. STRETCHING THE BUDGET

Most families have a budget from which to operate.

- Have a family meeting to discuss what can be done to help your family live within its budget.

- Make three suggestions to conserve money. Write your ideas below.

a. _____
   _____

b. _____
   _____

c. _____
   _____

- Put a star (✱) in front of the most important and practical suggestion.

- Devise a plan to put your budget suggestions into action.

- Tell about your family budget plan in the space below.

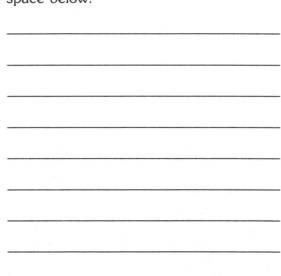

32. OFFERING HELP

- Discuss making a "help wanted" bulletin board on the family refrigerator.

- Ask each member of the family to fill out the daily request form.

- Ask each family member to meet at least one request daily.

- Tell about one request you made and one request you met in the space below.

Help! WANTED!

Date: _____

Need: _____

_____

Requested by: _____

Need met by: _____

Date: _____

Help! WANTED!

Date: _____

Need: _____

_____

Requested by: _____

Need met by: _____

Date: _____

- Discuss the value of your "help wanted" board with your classmates.

33. SOLVING FAMILY PROBLEMS

Increased cooperation within the family requires consistent effort on the part of each family member. Problems need solutions. Questions need answers.

- Write cooperative solutions to the family problems described below.

- Discuss with your teacher and classmates the advice you gave for each problem stated.

Dear Amber:

Since I am the oldest child, it seems that I have to do most of the housework. My parents expect very little from my younger brother and sister. What do you suggest?

Signed: Cinderella

Dear Cinderella:

_____

_____

_____

_____

Signed: Amber

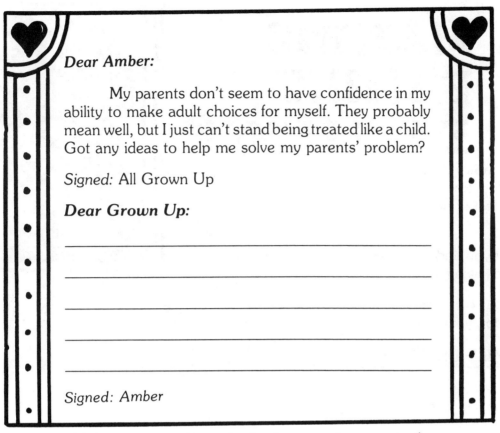

Dear Amber:

My parents don't seem to have confidence in my ability to make adult choices for myself. They probably mean well, but I just can't stand being treated like a child. Got any ideas to help me solve my parents' problem?

Signed: All Grown Up

Dear Grown Up:

_____

_____

_____

_____

_____

Signed: Amber

- Make your own **Dear Amber** letter and answer in the space provided.

Dear Amber:

_____

_____

_____

_____

Signed: _____

_____

_____

_____

_____

34. MAKING FAMILY DECISIONS

With each family decision comes a family responsibility. For instance, each member of the family is affected by the choice to have a family pet.

- Tell how you and your family might be affected by the following family decisions.

- Make your own decision and determine its effect upon your family.

EFFECT OF DECISION ON FAMILY

FAMILY DECISION

Mom decides to take on a full-time job outside the home.	→	

Family invites grandparent to visit for one month.	→	

	→	

35. JELLING ON THE JOB

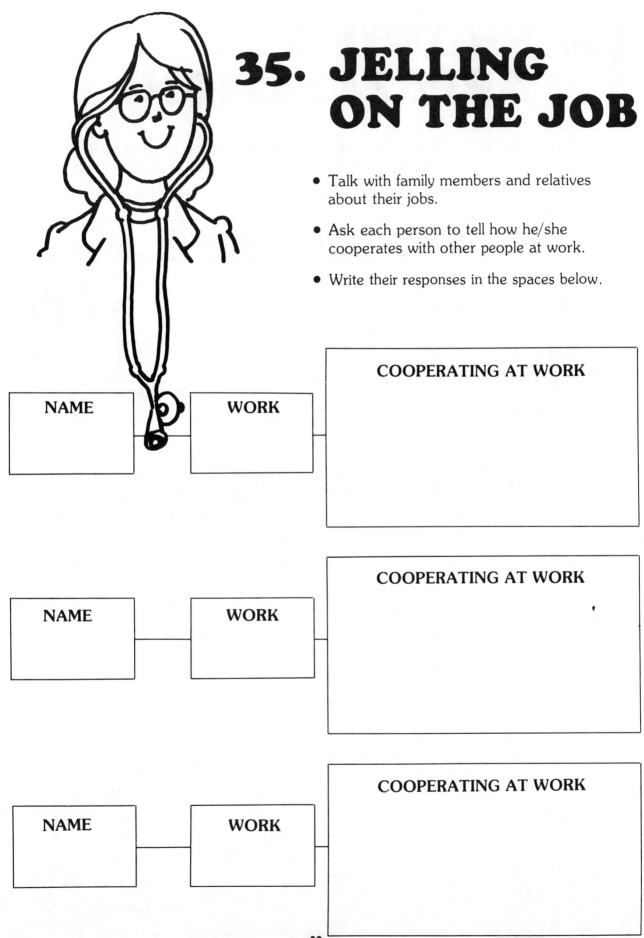

- Talk with family members and relatives about their jobs.

- Ask each person to tell how he/she cooperates with other people at work.

- Write their responses in the spaces below.

NAME	WORK	COOPERATING AT WORK

NAME	WORK	COOPERATING AT WORK

NAME	WORK	COOPERATING AT WORK

39

36. SHOWING APPRECIATION

You may want to show your appreciation to your family and relatives by completing the awards and giving them to various members of your family.

Appreciation Award

TO: _____
FOR: _____
FROM: _____
DATE: _____

Appreciation Award

TO: _____
FOR: _____
FROM: _____
DATE: _____

Appreciation Award

TO: _____
FOR: _____
FROM: _____
DATE: _____

SUMMARY: PART TWO COOPERATING WITH MY FAMILY

My family values:

_____

_____

_____

_____

I cooperate with my family:

☐ usually.

☐ often.

☐ sometimes.

☐ seldom.

☐ never.

My family can count on me to _____

_____

My family enjoys getting together for _____

_____

MEMBERS OF MY FAMILY	USUALLY	SOMETIMES	SELDOM
Spend quality time together.			
Pitch in and do the housework.			
Talk openly and listen attentively.			
Set rules and try to live by them.			
Work out problems as they come up.			
Enjoy being with one another.			

Name _____ Date _____

PART THREE: COOPERATING WITH MY FRIENDS AND CLASSMATES

PURPOSE:

The purpose of the activities in **PART THREE** is to assist you in becoming a more cooperative person with your friends and classmates.

Before beginning Part Three, complete the following statement:

I cooperate with my friends and classmates:

- ☐ usually.
- ☐ often.
- ☐ sometimes.
- ☐ seldom.
- ☐ never.

Name _____

Date _____

37. VALUING MY SCHOOL

Name of school:

_____

What I value most about my school:

a. _____

b. _____

c. _____

My classmates cooperate with one another by:

a. _____

b. _____

c. _____

I cooperate with my classmates by:

a. _____

b. _____

c. _____

38. FITTING TOGETHER

- Each student in the class has something unique and special to contribute to the group. Show how each member of the class fits together by following the directions for making a class puzzle.

Materials needed:

tag or poster board (36″ square)
scissors
magic markers
white glue
cardboard (36″ square)

Procedure:

a. Cut a large piece of poster board or tagboard into enough pieces for your classmates and teacher to have one piece.

b. On the puzzle piece have each person write the one special gift he/she brings to the class. Have each person sign his/her puzzle piece.

c. Have each person tell about his/her special talent.

d. Arrange the pieces of the puzzle until each fits together to make a total picture.

e. Glue the completed puzzle to a piece of cardboard.

f. Hang the puzzle in a special place of honor within the classroom or school.

- Write about a special quality that you bring to the class in the space below. Add your name to your unique gift.

_____

_____

_____

Joe Urbanski helps keep the classroom neat and clean.

Corinne Sanders is straight forward and honest with everyone.

Casey Crowley adds beautiful artwork around the classroom.

44

39. RECOGNIZING MY WORTH

- Tell about the unique gifts and talents you bring to your class.

- Listen to the unique gifts and talents that your classmates offer to one another.

- Complete the information below.

I, _____, bring
             Name

these special gifts and talents to my school community:

_____

_____

_____

_____

_____

_____

_____

_____

- Cut out the above information and paste it to a sheet of construction paper. Display the talents of each student in a special place within the clasroom.

lost in the woods
Jonathan

40. WORKING TOGETHER

- Think about the unique talents of your classmates.

- Write the names of the students with whom you would like to accomplish the following tasks. Choose many different people for assistance.

"If I were _____, I would want the help of _____ ."

planning a party   _____

lost in the woods   _____

writing a song   _____

behind in my math   _____

cooking a meal   _____

producing a play   _____

singing a song   _____

cleaning the yard   _____

playing baseball   _____

doing a science project   _____

_____   _____

_____   _____

_____   _____

41. OFFERING COUPONS

- Offer your assistance to your teacher and classmates.

- Fill out the free coupons and give them to people who would appreciate your assistance.

FREE COUPON FREE COUPON

TO: _____

OFFER GOOD FOR

_____

FROM: _____

GOOD THRU: _____

FREE COUPON FREE COUPON

TO: _____

OFFER GOOD FOR

_____

FROM: _____

GOOD THRU: _____

FREE COUPON FREE COUPON

TO: _____

OFFER GOOD FOR

_____

FROM: _____

GOOD THRU: _____

FREE COUPON FREE COUPON

TO: _____

OFFER GOOD FOR

_____

FROM: _____

GOOD THRU: _____

FREE COUPON FREE COUPON

TO: _____

OFFER GOOD FOR

_____

FROM: _____

GOOD THRU: _____

FREE COUPON FREE COUPON

TO: _____

OFFER GOOD FOR

_____

FROM: _____

GOOD THRU: _____

42. MIRRORING MOVEMENTS

In order to be a cooperative member of your class, it is necessary to be sensitive to those around you. The following activity is designed to increase your sensitivity to others.

Procedure:

Form in a circle of 12 to 15 students. Have one student stand in the center of the circle. The center student begins to move so that the other students can do the exact motions. Movements should be slow and simple. Take turns leading the group in mirroring the movements of others. (Note: This activity can be done with two people taking turns in leading each other through mirroring movements.)

Tell about your mirroring movements in the space provided. Describe your feelings of cooperation while participating in this activity.

_____

_____

_____

_____

_____

_____

_____

_____

_____

43. BUILDING TOGETHER

The following activity requires working together as a group. The activity is designed to show you how your actions affect the actions of others and vice versa.

Materials needed:

small-necked bottle

toothpicks

Procedure:

Six to eight people sit in a close circle. Each person has two toothpicks. Begin by one person placing one toothpick across the mouth of the bottle. Carefully pass the bottle to the next person, who also places the toothpick on the mouth of the bottle. Continue around the circle until all the players have successfully placed their toothpicks on the top of the bottle. If the toothpicks drop, repeat the procedure until the group is successful.

Tell about your experience in the space provided. Describe your feelings while participating in this activity.

_____

_____

_____

_____

_____

_____

_____

_____

_____

_____

44. BLOWING OFF STEAM

This activity requires working together as a group.

Materials needed:

paper cup
paper bag
table

Procedure:

Ask your classmates to kneel evenly around the table. Place the paper cup at one end of the table and the paper bag at the other end. At a given signal, join together in blowing the cup to the opposite end of the table. Work together until the cup drops into the bag. Do not touch the cup with your body. Repeat the procedure until you can quickly accomplish this feat.

Tell about your participation in this activity in the space provided.

_____

_____

_____

_____

_____

_____

_____

_____

_____

_____

_____

45. VOLLEYING TOGETHER

This activity changes the competitive game of volleyball to a cooperative group game.

Materials needed:

2 blankets
1 volleyball (or similar ball)
volleyball net

Procedure:

Form two groups of 8 to 10 people. Members of each group should place themselves evenly around the blanket on either side of the volleyball net. Place the volleyball in the center of one blanket. At the appropriate time, snap the blanket and allow the ball to fly over the net to be caught in the blanket of the opposite team. Pass the ball as rapidly and successfully as possible.

Describe your feelings of participation in this cooperative activity.

_____

_____

_____

_____

_____

_____

_____

_____

_____

_____

46. CREATING NEW GAMES

This activity challenges you and your friends to create a game which has no winners or losers.

Materials needed:

one ball of any size

Procedure:

Create a cooperative game using one ball and as many participants as you desire. Establish the goal of the game. Determine the rules. When you have created a game that you enjoy, teach another group of students how to play.

Write about your experience in the space below:

_____

_____

_____

_____

_____

_____

_____

_____

_____

_____

object:
balance ball
on head inside
Frisbee, walking
length of classroom.
Pass Frisbee and
ball onto next student.

47. COOPERATING IN A GROUP

- Name an organization to which you belong.

  _____

- Explain the goals and purpose of this organization.

  _____

- Tell how the members of this organization cooperate with one another to accomplish the goals of the organization.

  _____

  _____

  _____

  _____

  _____

- Evaluate the effectiveness of your organization by putting a check (✓) in the appropriate box.

	Usually	Sometimes	Seldom
The goals of the organization are accomplished.			
The members of the organization cooperate in accomplishing the goals of the organization.			

48. COOPERATING IN A CROWD

People are generally less cooperative in a crowd than with a group of friends. This is because no spirit of unity has been established within the crowd. Such unity has been established within a cooperative group.

- Put a **C** before the action if it is **cooperative**.

- Put a **U** before the action if it is **uncooperative**.

_____ Driver in line at a red light honks horn as soon as light turns green.

_____ Driver at red light motions for another driver to cut into the main line of traffic at change of traffic light.

_____ Elderly people are offered seats on a full bus.

_____ Children occupying seats on a full bus ignore the fact that elderly people are standing in the aisle.

_____ Airline offers to preboard parents traveling with small children.

_____ Airline announces general boarding without offering assistance to older and younger people.

_____ Shopper ignores small child trying to make purchase at counter.

_____ Shopper realizes small child has been waiting in line to pay and takes a place in line behind the child.

_____ Children push ahead of adults in line at an amusement park.

_____ Children wait their turn behind adults ahead of them at the amusement park.

54

49. KEEPING IN TOUCH

- Tell how you are a **cooperative** person in the space provided.

- Tell how you are an **uncooperative** person in the space provided.

Uncooperative Me!

Cooperative Me!

- Tell what you could do to be a more cooperative person.

_____

_____

50. COOPERATING WITH THE POLICE

Police officers are dedicated to protecting the citizens within a town or city.

- Ask a police officer to visit your classroom to discuss how you can cooperate with the police in making your neighborhood a safer place to live.
- List their suggestions in the space provided.

51. COOPERATING WITHOUT RULES

Our lives seem to be filled with family rules, school regulations, and government laws. Sometimes rules are seen as important and necessary to our well-being. Other times rules are seen as unnecessary restrictions on our freedom.

- Describe a coooperative way of living with as few rules as possible.

- What rules would be needed? Why?

52. CREATING YOUR FUTURE

A preferable future depends largely upon our ability to cooperate with one another today.

- Give your ideas as to how people might better work together to improve the following problems.

WATER SHORTAGE IN SUMMER MONTHS:

_____

_____

_____

_____

_____

VANDALISM OF THE SCHOOL BATHROOMS:

_____

_____

_____

SHORTAGE OF CANNED GOODS AT LOCAL FOOD BANK:

_____

_____

_____

_____

- State a local problem. Give a possible solution for this problem.

_____

_____

_____

_____

SUMMARY: PART THREE COOPERATING WITH MY FRIENDS AND CLASSMATES

I cooperate with my friends and classmates:

- ☐ usually.
- ☐ often.
- ☐ sometimes.
- ☐ seldom.
- ☐ never.

I cooperate with my classmates by:

_____

_____

_____

_____

_____

A special talent that I bring my school is:

_____

I appreciate _____ for his/her talent of

                     name of student

_____

Evaluation of Cooperative Games	Level of Enjoyment		
	High		Low
mirroring movements			
toothpick and bottle building			
blowing off steam			
blanket volleyball			
homemade game with no winners or losers			

Name _____ Date _____

FINAL SUMMARY

Cooperating means

_____

_____

_____

_____

I am generally:

☐ a competitive person.

☐ a cooperative person.

☐ both competitive
and cooperative.

I cooperate with my family by:_____

_____

My family can count on me to: _____

_____

A special talent I bring to my school is: _____

_____

I cooperate with my classmates by: _____

_____

	Usually	Often	Sometimes	Seldom	Never
I am a cooperative person.					
I cooperate with my family.					
I cooperate with my friends and classmates.					

Name _____

Date _____